CATS

Written By:
Herbert I. Kavet

Illustrated By:
Martin Riskin

Ivory Tower Publishing Co., Inc.
125 Walnut Street
P.O. Box 9132
Watertown, MA 02272-9132
Telephone #: (617) 923-1111   Fax #: (617) 923-8839

"Now that you put it that way, perhaps we could consider another book about cats."

"Would I be disturbing you?"

Finding A Kitten

The best way to get a kitten is to go into your most remote upstairs closet and whisper into the old coats stored there, "I think I'd like a kitten." By the time you return downstairs, six friends you didn't even know you had will have left messages on your answering machine offering kittens.

You may even be surprised and find a basket waiting by your back door.

"Now I want you two to be friends."

"That's another bad habit she learned from Fido."

Sleeping With Your Cat

Try sleeping with your cat and you'll realize why they nap all day. Cats are nocturnal animals and what seems so soft, relaxed and cuddly turns into an infuriating, constantly moving companion at night. Cats have the incredible ability to pussy foot across your head just as you're falling asleep.

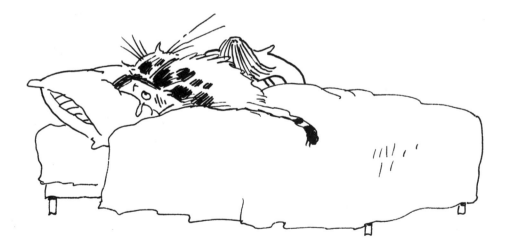

"Cat out?"

"You wouldn't be purring so contentedly if you knew you were getting fixed next week."

Living With Cat Hair

Cats have hair and cats will shed, so you'd *best* get used to it and work out a plan of action to minimize their effect on your life. Brushing your cat helps provided you can figure out where to dispose of a hair ball the size of Kansas. Daily vacuuming of your pet is even better if you can find four friends to hold pussy while you do it.

How To Live With Cat Hairs

1. Suggest your cat become an "outside" cat.

2. Limit your wardrobe to colors that blend with your cat's colors.

3. Apologize to all guests and brush them briskly.

4. Avoid swallowing hairs by learning to spit through teeth.

"Sam thinks it's the neighbor's cat."

"Muffy's been an inside cat her whole life."

What Cats Think About Pouncing On Their First Bird

The Cat Lady

Every neighborhood has one nice old lady who can always be counted on to take the strays children bring her and any unwanted kittens. These so-called cat ladies are federally chartered and required by law in most states.

Cleaning Your Cat

One of the great parts about owning a cat is that they clean themselves. By diligently licking off all the crap they accumulate in a day of crawling into invisible places, they transfer it all to their tongue which isn't too bad provided they don't lick you too often. All this cleaning does give some cats breath that can smell like an aging septic system.

Hair Balls

You don't have to clean your cat. Instead you get to clean up the hair balls they regurgitate which is one of the more disgusting jobs known to mankind.

"Whose dead bird is this?"

"Get real."

"I heard it, too."

"Do you like cats, Father?"

How To Tell If You've Got A Fat Cat

1. Naps on hood of car and leaves a dent
2. Cat's favorite chair sags
3. You have to change the kitty litter every 3 hours
4. If you can still pick up your cat, your hands sink in up to your wrists.

"Oh boy, reprocessed meat remnants in
artificial liver gravy!"

"Ah-ha! We've got him now."

"I guess she didn't feel a dead mouse was an
appropriate Mother's Day gift."

Timid Cats

1. Hides under furniture

2. Terrified of mice

3. Cringes when stroked

4. Pecks at food

5. Won't go near strangers

6. Terrified of thunderstorms

Aggressive Cats

1. Destroys furniture with impunity

2. Uses rodents for tennis balls

3. Bites fingers when tousled

4. Devours everything edible in sight and many things that are questionable

5. Strangers avoid house

6. Terrified of thunderstorms

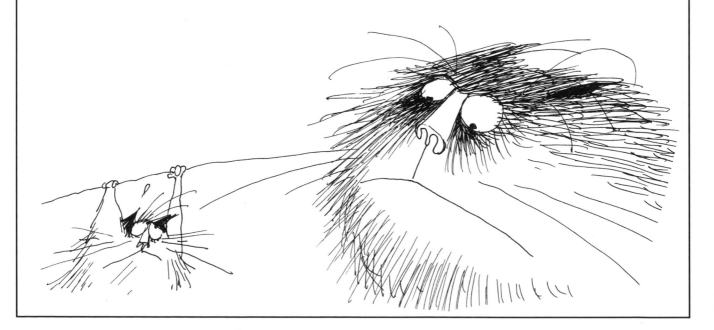

Why Cats Get Neurotic

"I'll be damned if they're going to fix me."

"You idiot."

Cat Myths

1. Cats can see in the dark.
2. Cats have nine lives.
3. Cats can always find their way home.
4. Cats always land on their feet.

"It seems the King of the Jungle is expecting
a thunderstorm."

"Health Inspector, you say?"

"So what's to discuss?..."

How To Recognize A Fussy Eater

1. Feigns disdain for contents of bowl

2. Sniffs food carefully as if to question sanity of someone giving them such stuff

3. Condescends to nibble only after being urged

4. Picks indifferently at food

"You can come out now, Smokey.
The landlord's gone."

"Relax, how will they know it was you?"

"Quick... Everybody look cute and adorable."

Fat Cats

There are only two ways to get a fat cat to lose weight. Feed it less, in which case the meowing will destroy your life, or encourage your pet to burn off more calories with exercise.

Activity	Calories Burned
Stalking mice	20 calories
Catching mouse	35 calories
Having to eat mouse	120 calories

Fat Cats

Activity	Calories Burned
Sitting on window sill	6 calories
If birds outside	65 calories
Chasing squirrel up tree	35 calories
If apartment on 20th floor	320 calories
Night out with the town cats	150 calories
Explaining the kittens	300 calories

"Sophie's been declawed."

"Put out a bowl of warm milk, Lady — we don't do cats up trees anymore."

"Well, that's everything. Now, where's Ghengis?"

Kitty Litter

<u>Advantages</u>

It keeps your cat's poo poo in one place.
It's easier than teaching your cat to use a toilet.
Once you lose your sense of smell, you'll hardly know it's there.

<u>Disadvantages</u>

It will put an end to walking barefoot in the bathroom.
The visual impact is something to be avoided at meal time.
Guests will never want to eat in your house.

"I didn't know cats shed."

"Kitty, where are you? We're going for a nice ride in the car."

"Karen thinks cats are sneaky."

Fleas

Flea collars, powders, and sprays will only control fleas, say, reducing them to about 2 million fleas per average cat. A typical cat will lick or claw to death about half of these on any given day, but the rest propagate at about 6 times that rate.

"Everybody hide, here comes the giant claw again."

"Usually he's very shy with strangers."

"Please, oh please."

Cat Farts

Here's a delicate subject. Admitting that a graceful feline animal like a cat is capable of farting is like thinking a beautiful little girl could fart. Well, cats can fart farts that will blow medium size birds out of a tree or bring tears to your eyes in a closed room, but they never give a sign or change their expression.

"Miss me?"

"It's something about a paternity suit."

Brushing

Brushing is a form of dieting all cats love best. Cats love to be brushed except when you get to the tangles in their fur, which is when they'll bite or claw you.

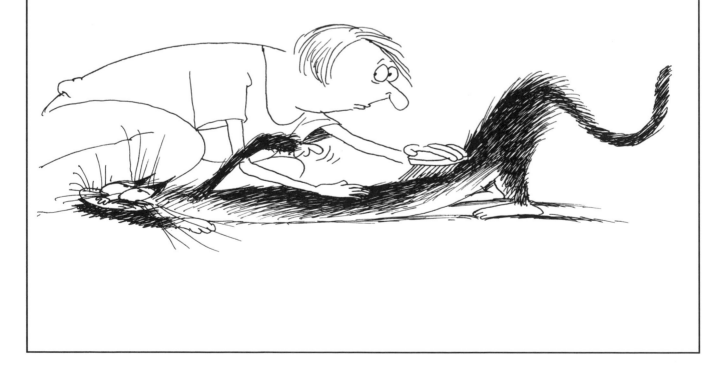

"When your stomach measures the same as
your tail, you're going on a diet."

Cat Food

How come your cat is rummaging around in the over-turned garbage can while her food bowl stands hardly nibbled? Do you think perhaps the ocean-fresh tuna intestines or chicken eviscerates with gland gravy are not quite as tasty as the TV ads promise? The FDA doesn't inspect cat food, you know, and since few owners taste the glop themselves, all the cat food companies have to worry about is that the smell doesn't rust the can opener.

"The cans, the cans. It's only 59¢ more."

"This is not a pretty sight."

Taffy tries to live 9 lives all at once.

These other books are available at many fine stores.

#2350 Sailing. Using the head at night • Sex & Sailing • Monsters in the Ice Chest • How to look nautical in bars and much more nautical nonsense.

#2351 Computers. Where computers really are made • How to understand computer manuals without reading them • Sell your old $2,000,000 computer for $60 • Why computers are always lonely and much more solid state computer humor.

#2352 Cats. Living with cat hair • The advantages of kitty litter • Cats that fart • How to tell if you've got a fat cat.

#2353 Tennis. Where do lost balls go? • Winning the psychological game • Catching your breath • Perfecting wood shots.

#2354 Bowling. A book of bowling cartoons that covers: Score sheet cheaters • Boozers • Women who show off • Facing your team after a bad box and much more.

#2355 Parenting. Understanding the Tooth Fairy • 1000 ways to toilet train • Informers and tattle tales • Differences between little girls and little boys • And enough other information and laughs to make every parent wet their beds.

#2356 Fitness. T-shirts that will stop them from laughing at you • Earn big money with muscles • Sex and Fitness • Lose weight with laughter from this book.

#2357 Golf. Playing the psychological game • Going to the toilet in the rough • How to tell a real golfer • Some of the best golf cartoons ever printed.

#2358 Fishing. Handling 9" mosquitoes • Raising worms in your microwave oven • Neighborhood targets for fly casting practice • How to get on a first name basis with the Coast Guard plus even more.

#2359 Bathrooms. Why people love their bathroom • Great games to help pass the time on toilets • A frank discussion of bathroom odors • Plus lots of other stuff everyone out of diapers should know.

#2360 Biking. Why the wind is always against you • Why bike clothes are so tight • And lots of other stuff about what goes thunk, thunk, thunk when you pedal.

#2361 Running. How to "go" in the woods • Why running shoes cost more than sneakers • Keeping your lungs from bursting by letting the other guy talk.

Ivory Tower Publishing Co., Inc. 125 Walnut St., PO Box 9132, Watertown, MA 02272-9132
Telephone #: (617) 923-1111 Fax #: (617) 923-8839